5 Minutes for World Peace ...Forever

A 90-Day Affirmation Plan

Ruth Fishel, M.Ed., C.A.C.
Illustrated by Bonny Van de Kamp

Health Communications, Inc.
Deerfield Beach, Florida

Other Books By Ruth Fishel:

Healing Energy: The Power Of Recovery
Time For Joy: Daily Affirmations
Learning To Live In The Now: 6-Week
    Personal Plan To Recovery
The Journey Within: A Spiritual Path To
    Recovery

Ruth Fishel
Spirithaven
1600 Falmouth Road
Centerville, MA 02632

© 1991 Ruth Fishel
ISBN 1-55874-169-0

Publisher: Health Communications, Inc.
            3201 S.W. 15th Street
            Deerfield Beach, FL 33442-8190

Dear Friends,

Welcome to *5 Minutes For World Peace . . . Forever.* I am very excited to have you participate in just 5 minutes a day to bring peace to this world and to let you know that you actually do have the power to make that happen.

The words that we speak and think are very powerful. Words can stimulate. Words can calm. Words can inspire. As individuals we are far more powerful than most of us realize. It has been proven that the power of thoughts actually change the chemicals in our brain affecting how we feel mentally and physically. Our thoughts are so powerful that they can and do affect those around us.

Spend a few moments being still and let yourself *feeel* how powerful one word can be.

Peace

Let yourself
feeeeeel
the effect of just one word

peace

Now imagine thousands of people reading that one word and the lasting effect that it would have on each individual as well as the people that they come in contact with.

Everything begins in the mind with a vision, a dream, a thought. A new book, a building, a community all begin with the thought of a book, a building, a community and then become a reality.

World Peace Can Begin
With The Thought Of World Peace
And Then Become A Reality.

- Each page of this book is filled with inspirational thoughts, words and quotes from famous and not so famous people. Each page of this book represents one day.
- Spend just five minutes each day being with the thoughts on the page.
- Think about them. Sit quietly with them. Meditate on them.
- Let the feelings of the words fill you with peace and strength.
- And then carry that feeling with you for the rest of your day, sharing it with others.
- Imagine the potential for peace when hundred of thousands of people . . . a page at a time, a day at a time . . . pass that feeling on to others.

- Imagine how extremely powerful it can be.

Thank you for joining me and all the others who are passing on the power of thought, prayer and meditation so that the horrors of war can cease and there can be peace for all human beings.

In Peace and Love,
Ruth Fishel

THIS IS PROBABLY THE MOST POWERFUL TOOL FOR PEACE YOU HAVE EVER HAD IN YOUR HANDS.

There are 1,440 minutes in a day.
That means there are 86,400 seconds.
I can afford to contribute 5 minutes to world
    peace.
I can afford to contribute 300 seconds to
    world peace.
That leaves 1,435 minutes for me.
That leaves 86,100 seconds for me.
I can afford to be that generous.

5 minutes
for World Peace
... forever

*There are two ways
of spreading light:
to be the candle
or the mirror that reflects it.*

Edith Wharton

I absolutely do make a difference in this
world.
Every thought, feeling and action I have
makes a difference.
I can change one negative thought,
feeling or action
to a positive one today
And make a positive difference in this
world.

Write the word *peace* on a piece of paper, a small stone or a shell. Then put it in your pocket.

Know that you are carrying *peace* with you wherever you go.

Know that whatever comes up for you during the day, you always have *peace* with you.

Try this. It is amazing how just this five-letter word *peace* can change a mood, an argument, an upset . . .

the world.

peaceful pockets...

Sometime they'll give a war and
nobody will come.

Carl Sandburg
The People, Yes

I can give this day everything I have. I can give my utmost attention and volition to at least 5 minutes today, meditating for peace in the world. I can carry this thought, this feeling with me and express it in all my actions to the best of my ability for the rest of the day.

I can feel the great power of the thought that I am joining with so many others with the same intention.

Today I will do my very best to bring peace to my life and to the lives of those around me.

5

In the Middle East there is a legend of a little sparrow lying on its back in the middle of the road. A horseman comes by, dismounts and asks the sparrow why it is lying upside down like that.

"I hear the heavens are about to fall today," says the sparrow.

"Oh," says the horseman, "and I suppose your puny legs can hold up the heavens?"

"One does what one can," replies the sparrow. "One does what one can."

*holding up
the heavens with joy!*

It isn't enough to talk about peace.
One must believe in it.
One must work at it.

Eleanor Roosevelt

Not one human being in this world
should be suffering.
Not one person should be hungry.
Not one person should be homeless.
Not one person should be lonely.

The world deserves peace today.

*Today I am doing all I can to make sure
peace is happening in the world.*

hope

At least 5 minutes . . .
now
To find at least one thing that I have
to be thankful for.

At least 5 minutes . . .
now
To let my heart fill.

At least 5 minutes . . .
now
To feel full.

At least 5 minutes . . .
To feel *full*
of
peace

When I am at peace,
  the world is a very peaceful place to be.
When I am at peace,
  peace is all I see.

Submitted by
Joan Scudder
Mother, Windsurfer,
Runner, Artist, Friend

Conflict will inevitably arise so long as there is a division between "what should be" and "what is," and any conflict is a dissipation of energy.

J. Krishnamurti

Be one

Today I will see things as they are, not as I would like them to be. I will pray for acceptance of what is. I can find real peace in the substance of truth and reality, not in fantasies and daydreams.

With this energy I can feel my inner strength and carry on my mission of peace.

Nobody could make a greater mistake
than he who did nothing because he could
only do a little.

Edmund Burke

Today I am going deep within me to find
   my strength.
Today I am going deep within me to find
   the very best of me that I can offer to at
   least one other human being to make the
   world a better place to be.

finding my strength
within me!

I am finding my own goodness and acting on it,
knowing I have something to offer
to this world for peace.

And they shall
beat their
swords
into
plowshares,
And their spears
into
pruninghooks:
Nation shall not
lift up sword
against nation,
neither
shall they
learn
war
anymore.

Isaiah 2:4.

I am just one of many
meditating for world peace today.
I am just one of many
making a contribution in the world today.
I am neither less nor more,
but an important *one*,
and that gives me a great deal
of peace and joy.

*Man must evolve for all human
conflict a method which rejects revenge,
aggression and retaliation.
The foundation of such a method is love.*

Martin Luther King, Jr.

At some level I know that every person in
this entire world is my family.
I am opening more and more to this
realization and allowing myself to feel
this connection deep within me.
I am holding my world family gently
in my heart today.
I am sending thoughts of peace and love
to my world family
today.

We look forward to the time when the power of love will replace the love of power. Then will the world know the blessings of peace.

William Ewart Gladstone

I have great power today . . . the power of
  my mind.
I can sit and think about this power and
  guide it to thoughts of peace.
I can think about peace for all the people in
  the world for 5 minutes today.
I can encourage someone else to think
  about peace for all the people
  in the world today.

. . . And together we can make that
  happen.

I always found
that if I pray in the morning
as if everything
depends upon God,
and then go out and work
as if everything
depends upon
me,
blessings
come beyond
all telling.

If we triumph
in the little things
of our
common hours
and continue to be
dedicated
and have a positive
attitude,
we should all
triumph
in our lives.

Jeanne Dixon

Peace be my Prayer

I stand in the rain in front of the White House. My placard for Peace has disintegrated. I have signed one hundred damp petitions to the President. Now, with the rain pouring down my neck, I am face to face with despair. Discouraged, I can do no more. All I can do now is let the tears roll down my cheeks as I hand it over to my Higher Power. I give it to You, God, Yahweh, Allah, the Goddess. I admit I am powerless. Only my Higher Power can restore the world to sanity. And as I stand here tearfully surrendering my all, the rain stops and the sun breaks through the clouds. God has heard my prayer. Look . . . there's a rainbow!

Submitted by
Marie Stilkind
Mother-Grandmother,
Jewish Quaker Pacifist,
Editor

Every one of us reading this page today has the power of our intention in common. Let's focus on that intention right now. Each individual's intention for peace is so powerful that it actually changes our energy. This energy is so powerful that it changes the way we feel and the way we act.

Focus on that energy and let your thoughts expand to all of us. The energy from our collective intention is so powerful it is changing the world at this very moment.

Today I focus on peace,
knowing I am connected with the energies of
millions of other people focused on peace.

Often in my greatest struggles I find my self-will running neck and neck with powerlessness. I always win when I recognize the hopelessness of such a race and willingly yield to my competition.

I then know peace.

Submitted by
Rosalie
Educator and Student

If you can, help others; if you cannot do that,
at least do not harm them.

Randy Rind quoted in
Chop Wood, Carry Water

My day is a success if I harm no one.
My day is more successful if I harm no one
   and accomplish one peaceful action for
   myself.
My day is even more successful if I harm
   no one, accomplish one peaceful action
   for myself and accomplish one peaceful
   action for at least one other human
   being.

Knowing that I am connected with others
who are *thinking* about world peace in this
moment is an electrifying idea.
I let this *energy* flow through me,
awakening all the sleeping places of my soul.
I am *alive* in this connection,
sending
this *energy*
in this moment
now
to all those in the *universe* who need it.

The more I work with people and the more I go through life, the more I realize that people just want to be happy. If I take 5 minutes out of each day to remember to treat people the same way I want to be treated, we could accomplish wonderful things together.

Submitted by
Bob Fishel
Manager, Son, Friend, Brother,
Creative Thinker, Problem-
Solver, Photographer

together we can!

TODAY I HONOR MYSELF

I honor myself as a unique human being.
I honor my similarities to
    and my differences from others.
I honor all that I like and all that I do not
    like about myself.
I honor all that I know and all that I have
    not yet discovered about myself.
And I even honor that which I hide from
    myself.
I honor my past and all I have experienced
    in my past that has brought me to
    where I am today . . .
A step closer to honoring
    all the sameness and
    differences in others.
            . . . A step closer to peace.

In this moment, I slow down enough to be with myself.

In this moment, I slow down enough to connect with a power greater than myself.

In this moment, I am deeply connected with many other people who have slowed down to make this same connection.

Slowly . . .

   I let myself . . .

      feeeel . . .

         that connection.

           I am not alone.

The Bible teaches
quite unequivocally that
people are
created for fellowship,
or togetherness:
not for
alienation,
apartness,
enmity
and
division.

Archbishop Desmond Tutu

There is a natural state present in me, undisturbed and still. I find it at the core of who I am. When I quiet myself and move my focus, awareness and consciousness away from external distractions and separations, I find within me strength, calm and stability. I find a peaceful and loving essence.

I pray that I move to this place and essence often . . . that I let this be the source of my activities, emotions, thoughts, choices and communications.

I pray that I do this well enough so this peace and loving become contagious.

I pray that enough people share their loving and that — one by one — this peace will reach to all mankind.

Submitted by
Terry Tillman
Author, Publisher,
Photographer, Ski Instructor,
Ambassador of Peace:
Institute for Individual
and World Peace

When the Nazis came for the Jews, I didn't speak out because I wasn't a Jew. When they came for the Communists, I didn't speak out because I wasn't a Communist. When they came for the Trade Unionists, I didn't speak out because I wasn't a Trade Unionist. Then they came for me and there was no one left to speak out for me.

Martin Niemoller

Today I have the courage to walk through any fear and speak up when I can make a difference. Today I know that my voice counts as one — and one is a very powerful number.

*Peace
cannot be
kept by force.
It
can only
be
achieved by
understanding.*

Albert Einstein

Sitting quietly today, I am going deep within my heart to find that place where we are all connected . . .

That place called love.

Words have the power to
move us from a place
very deep within us.
Words have the power to
shift us from old beliefs to
new ones.
Words have the power to
inspire us to take action steps that
make a difference.
Words have the power to
shake us up and
help us change.
Words have the power to
touch our hearts and
make us feel differently.

*Today I am being mindful of the words I speak
and the words I think. I am aware of what I hear
and who I talk to. I know that words make a
difference. I am putting my energy into positive,
loving and peace-producing words today.*

There is many a boy here today who looks on war as all glory but, boys, it is all hell. You can bear this warning voice to generations to come. I look upon war with horror.

General William T. Sherman's
speech to war veterans, 1880

Today I find ways to release all anger and resentments that I am holding onto from the past so I can be free to experience peace in this moment.

I can write a letter that I will or will not mail.

I can talk to a friend, family member, clergy, spiritual adviser or therapist.

I can make an amend if it is appropriate.

I can do a good deed.

I can pray and meditate.

I can ask for help and trust that help is on the way.

We will have peace only when we are as aggressive in the pursuit of peace as we are in the pursuit of war.

Submitted by
Sandy Bierig
Mom, Grandmom, Author,
Activist, Teacher

*They could only be as fast
as the slowest member of the caravan.*

> Written on a rock on the side of a
> mountain by someone from the
> Coronado Expedition in the 1500s

*Today I will take this time of quiet to search for
the strengths I have to offer others. I will focus on
my strengths and feel their power, knowing I can
spread this power as a force of energy for peace
and freedom.*

Because I do not agree with someone does not mean I have to hate him, be against him or fight with him.

Because someone is coming from a different place does not make either of us right or wrong. It just means that we are in different places.

I am spending a few moments today considering how I differ from other people, reflecting on the varieties of experiences and personalities that make up human nature.

The only devils in this world are those run-ning around in our own hearts, and that is where all our battles should be fought.

Mahatma Gandhi

[We] sought through prayer and meditation to improve our conscious contact with God, as we understood God, *praying only for God's will for us and the power to carry that out.*

> Step 11 (adapted) from the 12 Steps of Alcoholics Anonymous

I am so grateful to everyone who has stopped for this moment to think about world peace.

I am so grateful to everyone who is out there taking this time so that we all join spiritually to reach this common goal.

I am so grateful that together we *can* make a difference.

Even when
I have doubt, I know
that
a power greater
than myself
is guiding
me
on my
spiritual path
to peace
today.

*I do not want
the peace
that passeth
understanding,
I want
the
understanding
which
bringeth
peace.*

Helen Keller

When we discover the still quiet place that lies within each of us, we can see it as a base to untangle ourselves from the doubt, indecision, ill health, guilt and other forms of old programming that result in confused and defused actions.

Hallie Iglehart

Miracles begin to happen when we sit still and look within. Let those miracles be there for you today. As you dare to see that you have been ruled by old programming, know that new truths — positive, healthy thoughts — are taking its place. Know that you are in the process of moving forward. And in the process you are helping others in this universe to move forward.

I am clearing out old confusion and doubt so I can see the miracles today and participate in the recovery of the universe.

___

*All that I am is a result of
what I have thought.*

The Dhammapada

Humanity has wandered so far, thinking love and peace were something we would get when we arrived somewhere or acquired or accomplished something. Today we can learn to slow down.

Today we can learn a new truth. Stop for a moment and think *"peace,"* and let that thought pour over you.

Stop for a moment and think *"love,"* and let those feelings pour over you.

Wherever you are, whatever you are doing, at any time in any day, just stop for a moment. You will find *peace* and *love.* Whatever you choose to think, to feel, to have, to be . . . is yours . . . whenever you choose it.

*Today I take the time to be with me and find
peace and love and truth. It is mine if
I just stop. It is mine if I just think the
thoughts I want to feel.*

Today I will know that peace is the child of justice, that peace is more than the absence of war.

Submitted by Diane Crosby, Nurse. Found in her church bulletin without author's name.

Peacework

*Empathy frees me from fear for I
know others are nearby.*

Arthur Dobrin

All breath becomes one breath.
Everyone's pulse beats together.
Today.
Now.
In this moment.
We are one.

In troubled times it is hard to feel peaceful.
In difficult times it is hard to feel peaceful.

I can take 5 minutes to allow myself to be
with thoughts of peace, no matter what I
am going through today.

I can take 5 minutes and fill myself with
peaceful energy, no matter what else I am
feeling today.

> *Today I am taking 5 minutes to give*
> *to thoughts of peace, no matter what*
> *is going on in my world.*

Peace is better than war because in peace the sons bury their fathers, but in war the fathers bury their sons.

Roger Bacon

As we meditate together each day, I am beginning to feel closer to those of you who are joined with me in this commitment for *peace*. Today I stop and take time to feel your energy as it reinforces my commitment.

I don't know you and yet I know you.

I don't see you and yet I feel you.

I know what is in your hearts.

I know the goodness of your intentions.

And I know your fears.

Together . . . we make a powerful force for peace.

Today I gather my strength from all the people in this world who are passing on the message for peace and love.

The key to a passionate life is to trust and follow the energy within us.

Shakti Gawain

As we begin to slow down . . . to take this time each day . . . we begin to quiet our minds. In this process we discover the very traits that have blocked our energy. We come face to face with our fears, our resistance and our denial. As we accept what we see, without judgment but with gratitude, we can actually feel new energies being released. Trust this new energy. It is part of a bigger picture, a higher level of spirituality. It will bring change on a grander scale to a world that so badly needs it.

Today I am willing to let go of all the negative tapes that block me from my truth. As I let go, I trust and follow a powerful new energy that is guiding me and all the world's people to a higher purpose.

All humankind is in the midst of this huge evolutional Power. When the collective unconscious begins a new stage in this process, it tolerates no obstacle. In order to force a new ideal or possibility into the conscious psyche of the people, it will turn a society upside down, launch crusades, beget new religions or shake empires down into rubble.

Robert Johnson

Evolve ♡ ♡ ♡
love

Day 50

Peace is a lot like fertilizer . . . you have to spread it around to do any good. And the more places you spread it, the more likely any number of seeds will take root and grow.

Submitted by
Michael E. Miller
Publishing Executive

Today I will spread peace and love everywhere I go. Today I will smile more and say kind words to everyone I meet. Today I will make a conscious effort to like everyone, not just my loved ones.

*Internationalism does not mean
the end of individual nations. Orchestras
don't mean the end of violins.*

Golda Meir
Former Prime Minister of Israel

**Today I will sing a love song to
the world that will echo throughout
the universe forever.**

*Anyone who chooses to live his life
in loving can change the world.*

John-Roger

We have tried everything else but love. We have tried wars, torture, confinement, deprivation, restrictions, embargoes, imprisonment, rules and regulations, discrimination, laws and so on.

Has the whole world ever tried love for just one day?

Today I will do my best to bring love to everything I do, everyone I meet and every thought I think. I can feel the power of this thought as it is carried out by all who are reading this page today.

There are times when I have to separate myself from certain people, places and things in order to feel at peace.

There are times when I have to create a distance between myself and certain people, places and things in order to find peace in my heart.

This does not mean they are right or wrong or I am right or wrong. It just means we are not right for each other at this particular time. It does not mean forever. It means for now.

It is okay to choose, whenever possible, the people, places and things I have in my life for this day so that I can be at peace.

sometimes....

I have known war as few men now living know it. Its very destructiveness on both friend and foe has rendered it useless as a means of settling international disputes.

General Douglas MacArthur

If we could read the secret history of our "enemies," we should find in each man's and woman's life sorrow and suffering enough to disarm all hostility.

Henry Wadsworth Longfellow

Meditation is a form of acknowledging your connection with the spirit of universal love, and it allows a sense of peace and love to flood your being. The tranquility that follows stays with you, reducing stress and promoting a state of awareness throughout the day.

Ruth Ross
Prospering Woman

As we let ourselves relax and let stress leave our bodies, we open up to more and more tranquility and peace. The more we open and let go of our stress, the more room we make to be filled with peace and love, and we carry that with us throughout our day.

As I stop today and take the time to be still, I get in touch with my Higher Power. I feel myself filling with love and peace as I relax and let go of the stress in my day, and I pass this peace on to others.

*Creating more human suffering
is no longer an option.*

As I improve my own abilities to communicate more clearly, my relationships will be healthier.

As my personal relationships become healthier, peace will improve in my world.

And as each of us raises our own awareness to clear and peaceful communications, the world becomes healthier.

We can talk now instead of fight.

Energy

The peace in the world depends on how well we raise our children. If all children grow up loved, the love will permeate the world and the destructive, addictive behavior will cease. We may need to license parents to reach this condition.

Submitted by
Dr. Bernie S. Siegel

Imagine an invisible silk thread connecting all of us who are committed to peace. Now imagine the energy of our thoughts and the power from our intention for peace flowing through it, expanding to everyone who is near it.

And now imagine that energy touching everyone within miles of our invisible thread.

Know that the entire world is a bit brighter, a bit richer, more full of love because we have spent at least these five minutes committed to world peace.

Mankind must put an end to war or war will put an end to mankind . . . . War will exist until the distant day when the conscientious objector enjoys the same reputation and prestige that the warrior does today.

John F. Kennedy

Most people fail because they do not wake and see when they stand at the fork in the road and have to decide.

Erich Fromm

Today we know that we have choices.
. . . We can take a stand.
. . . We can say *yes*.
. . . We can say *no*.
. . . We can stop and wait for inner
  guidance.
. . . We can take whatever steps are
  necessary for peace.

We can make a difference!

God grant me the
Serenity
To accept the things I cannot change,
Courage
to change the things I can,
And wisdom
to know the difference.

Serenity Prayer
Adapted from
Reinhold Niebuhr

Today I have the wisdom to know that I can change this world by changing me. By bringing peace to me, I bring peace to this world.

☆

I breathe softly into myself,
  bringing awareness to any pain I am
  feeling in this moment.
I take this time now to stop and listen to any
  emotional or physical discomfort I have.
I pray that I do not act or speak out of my
  own pain with the intention of hurting
  anyone else.

Triumph is just "umph" added to "try."

Anonymous advertisement

If I spread the word of peace to two people, then three of us have it. If we three each spread it to two more people, and those six each spread it to two more people, and then those six each spread it to two people, in a short time it will reach 12, then 24, then 48, then 96, which will equal 192 and soon 384, 768, 1536, 3072, and soon . . .

Peace will
triumph
throughout the world!

We limit ourselves by thinking that things can't be done. Many think peace in the world is impossible — many think that inner peace cannot be attained. It's the one who doesn't know it can't be done who does it!

Peace Pilgrim

Peace Pilgrim devoted her entire life to the cause of peace, walking the country endlessly, talking to anyone wanting to listen. I only need spend these few minutes facing in the direction of peace to add my intention to hers.

peace and joy...

It is a little embarrassing that after 45 years of research and study, the best advice I can give to people is to be a little kinder to each other.

> Aldous Huxley
> Quote submitted by
> Tom Steven Kirkman
> Poet, Quaker,
> Recovering Person With AIDS

Today I will be a little kinder to everyone I meet.

MAKE SOUP NOT WAR

When life begins whirling out of control, I slow myself down by making soup. This is what I did the night U.S. planes began bombing Iraq. Aside from being therapeutic to prepare, that soup was delicious and healthy and everyone who ate it felt loved and nurtured.

> Submitted by
> Gina Ogden
> Psychotherapist,
> Writer, Maker of Soup

Today I will slow myself down and center myself by doing something that brings me peace and serenity. Today I will take the time to do something nurturing and healthy, bringing full mindfulness to each moment and each action.

just as I am

Perseverance is a great element of success. If you only knock long enough and loud enough at the gate, you are sure to wake up somebody.

Henry Wadsworth Longfellow

What I give, I get back multiplied
If I give love, I am loved.
If I give joy, I am joyful.
If I give peace, I am peaceful.
I receive as I give.

Submitted by
Carol Ann Friel
Mom, Health Teacher

START HERE

Love
ever
lasting

There is
no
way
to peace.
Peace
is
the
way.

A.J. Muste

Peace!

If I am still carrying old anger, old resentments or old pain, I pray for them to be removed today so that I can experience freedom.

Today I know that the more strongly I feel freedom, the more strongly I feel peaceful and the more strongly I pass peace on to others.

letting go

thanks

NAMASTE

I honor the place in you in which the entire universe dwells. I honor the place in you which is of love, of truth, of light and of peace. When you are in that place in you, and I am in that place in me, we are one.

Found on a greeting card by
Ingrid Peterson

More and more of us know this is the time to speak and the time of peace is growing. Our strength and power are gaining. Our energy is joining and spreading. Today we can feel that power and shout it out to others. We can pass it on.

SHOUTING ABOUT LOVE!

go ahead!

*When you have accepted your mission to extend
peace you will find peace, for by making it
manifest, you will see it.*

A Course In Miracles

Today I bring my awareness to every living thing and being I see, feel, hear, touch,
taste and smell.

I take time to let myself fill with the won-
der of all the growth and beauty in this
world. I take time to find a tree or a flower,
a bird, an ant, a shell or a blade of grass and
just be there with it for a moment or
two . . . marveling at the process.

I know that I share this life with all beings
in all corners of the world.

All civilization has been on a journey that has arrived right here, right now, in this moment in time and space.

Everything we did was necessary to get to where we are. We have come so far.

We are ready to take the next step on our spiritual journey, to experience and accept *peace* and *freedom* in our lives and to pass them on to others. We are participants in the spiritual transformation of civilization. Together we have the power to make this happen.

Today I am participating in the spiritual transformation of civilization.

Today the real test of power is not capacity
to make war but capacity to prevent it.

Anne O'Hare McCormack

finding peace in our lives
requires love.

The power for love and peace is in all people.
Today I will find ways to use mine.

Lord,
make us
instruments
of Thy
peace.

Where there is hatred,
let us sow love;

Where there is injury,
pardon;

Where there is discord,
union;

Where there is doubt,
faith;

Where there is despair,
hope;

Where there is darkness,
light;

Where there is sadness,
joy.

St. Francis of Assisi

What can I do to make a difference today?
As I sit here in this 5 minutes that I have committed to world peace, I can discover at least one thing that will change my life and thus affect the lives of those around me.
It does not have to be big or great.
One thing to make my life more peaceful.
Just one thing.
One small thing.
I *do* make a difference!

Today I know any action I make that comes from peace and love has a rippling effect upon the entire world.

I think that people
want peace
so much that
one of
these days
government had
better get out
of the way
and let
them
have
it.

Dwight D. Eisenhower

If I could add anything
[to this peace book],
it would be
to urge all of us
to try
to build a
United Nations
that can
truly create a
new world order.
I think we have the best
opportunity to
build that
kind of U.N.
we have
ever had in our
lifetime.

Submitted by
Former Massachusetts
Governor and Democratic
Presidential Nominee
Michael J. Dukakis

Why, of course, people don't want war. Why should some poor slob on a farm want to risk his life in a war when the best he can get out of it is to come back to his farm in one piece? Naturally the common people don't want war: neither in Russia, nor in England, nor for that matter in Germany. That is understood. But after all, it is the leaders of a country who determine the policy, and it is always a simple matter to drag the people along, whether it is a democracy or a fascist dictatorship or a parliament or a communist dictatorship. Voice or no voice, the people can always be brought to the bidding of the leaders. That is easy. All you have to do is tell them that they are being attacked, and denounce the pacifists for lack of patriotism and exposing the country to danger. It works the same in any country.

Hermann Goering
At the Nuremberg Trials

*Don't quit before
the
miracle
happens.*

Expression heard around
12-Step recovery programs

Peace is the miracle.
Wait.
It is happening.

Day 82

Today I will quiet my mind
and get in touch with the
universal energy that is in all of us.
I know that universal energy
is directing all of us
toward peace.

Gentle . . .
Soft . . .

I spend these five minutes gently
breathing into all
the lines and angles of my body,
filling myself with softness and
peace.

I will do my very best to deal with
whatever comes up today
with gentleness and softness.

All that is needed for evil to flourish is for good people to remain silent.

Author unknown

*I am beginning to feel my own
personal power today.
I am moved to express myself whenever
I can make a difference
for peace.*

*Love is the rare herb that makes a friend
even of a sworn enemy and this herb
grows out of nonviolence.*

Mahatma Gandhi

When we carry peace in our hearts,
we find joy.

*Today I will do something nice for a friend . . .
make a thermos of soup or send a homemade card
or visualize my friend in a healing white light
that covers the whole world as well . . . including
you.*

The longest journey is the journey inward, for he who has chosen his destiny has started upon his quest for the source of his being.

Dag Hammarskjold

We have often looked to other people, places and things for answers. We thought others could free the world of wars, pain, pollution, starvation, disease, homelessness and ignorance.

It is time to begin to trust that small voice within, coming from the people we really are. It is time to look within and begin to uncover our own strength and wisdom. It is time to discover our own power and participate in the healing of our world.

Peace among the parts is essential for peace throughout the world. War is a product of materialism and need for power. Let me begin to simplify my life through reducing my wants and possessions. Let me not forget the importance of quality relationships with family and friends and that treating all people with respect maintains my dignity.

Submitted by
Ellen Harris Winans
Gallery Owner

*May any peace that dwells in my heart not be
an easy peace that comes from not caring
enough. May it rather be a peace that emerges
from wrestling with the pain and darkness
that is within my own heart and in the heart
of the world.*

Submitted by Muriel Wilson
Prayer Circle Secretary
Iona Community,
Argyll, Scotland

We need to continue this on-going journey
to self-exploration and discover to the tiniest
detail all that we can let go of to come to
peace in our hearts. There can be no room
for anger, resentments or lack of forgiveness
of our self or any other person. It is in the
willingness to undertake it, not the comple-
tion of this search, that makes peace possible.

*Today I continue to take personal inventory so
that I may be aware of the changes that I must
make so that my inner world will be a place of
peace and serenity.*

I am listening to the voice of
Truth and Love and Peace
within myself today.
I feel
Peace
pouring over my body
as I prepare myself for this day.
I am so grateful
for all the people
who join me
in making Peace a reality
in our time.